Keystone
Habits

Bestselling author **Steven Schuster** has always been captivated by the intricacies of the human mind. From the echoing hallways of libraries to the serene landscapes of the Rocky Mountains, Steven has ventured far and wide in his relentless quest for knowledge and first-hand experience. Blending profound psychological insights with captivating storytelling, he has reached readers across the globe, igniting their passion for self-discovery.

A self-proclaimed "eternal student", Steven spends his days immersed in a medley of fictional prose and cutting-edge research, distilling wisdom that spans different fields of study.

When he's not penning transformative books, you'll find Steven exploring a hidden forest trail, indulging in his love for vintage jazz, or lost in deep conversation with fellow thinkers at quaint cafés from Paris to Kuala Lumpur.

Join Steven on a journey into the depths of consciousness, and emerge with knowledge that help you live your best life.

Keystone Habits

Unleash an avalanche-like change in your life

STEVEN SCHUSTER

RUPA

Published by
Rupa Publications India Pvt. Ltd 2024
7/16, Ansari Road, Daryaganj
New Delhi 110002

Sales centres:
Bengaluru Chennai
Hyderabad Jaipur Kathmandu
Kolkata Mumbai Prayagraj

Copyright © Steven Schuster 2024
Published under arrangement with Steven Schuster through
TLL Literary Agency.

The views and opinions expressed in this book are the author's
own and the facts are as reported by him which have been
verified to the extent possible, and the publishers are not in
any way liable for the same.

All rights reserved.
No part of this publication may be reproduced, transmitted,
or stored in a retrieval system, in any form or by any means, electronic,
mechanical, photocopying, recording or otherwise, without the prior
permission of the publisher.

P-ISBN: 978-93-5702-804-2
E-ISBN: 978-93-5702-938-4

First impression 2024

10 9 8 7 6 5 4 3 2 1

The moral right of the author has been asserted.

Printed in India

This book is sold subject to the condition that it shall not, by way of
trade or otherwise, be lent, resold, hired out, or otherwise circulated,
without the publisher's prior consent, in any form of binding or
cover other than that in which it is published.

Contents

Introduction vii

1. Self-Discipline 1
2. Take Risks 10
3. Focus 20
4. Lifelong Learning 28
5. The Law of Attraction 39
6. Mindfulness 46
7. Meditation 51
8. Have Something to Wake Up For 60
9. Saving and Budgeting 66

Final Words... 80

References 81

Endnotes 83

Introduction

If you look at any bookstore in the self-help section, the word "habits" is going to jump out time and time again. If you are walking down the street, you will see plenty of billboards talking about overcoming your bad habits, your addictions, and your shortcomings. Different strategies to change our habits or change them completely bombard us day after day. There are so many options, suggestions, tips, and tricks, so many different habits to adopt, that it may be overwhelming to even think about them. So very often we just resign and shrug our shoulders. "I can't do it. I wish I could, but I'd have so much to change about myself that I already know I'm set up to fail."

Have you ever felt this way? I'm sure you wish to be able to maintain a healthy lifestyle, which involves healthy eating habits, regular exercise, meditation, regular meaningful communication with loved ones, a digital detox, a decluttered environment, punctuality, a stress-averse mindset, and so on. I bet you want to be your best self at home, at work, in your community, in your faith … and there is an abundance of suggestions on which habits to adopt to achieve all of those. In maintaining a healthy lifestyle, I listed eight habits, and my list wasn't exhaustive at all. Eight habits there, eight habits for good relationships, eight habits for work ... Who would even want to get started in adopting them? It feels like running a lifetime marathon to be "our best selves."

On one hand, yes, life is a long stretch of striving to grow, to learn, to improve. But we don't need to be overwhelmed by its magnitude. There are some shortcuts—even when it comes to good habits—we can learn and use to our benefit. This book is about those shortcuts.

Let me present what I'm talking about with learning to drive. When you're sixteen to eighteen, depending where you're from, you decide that you want to get your driver's license. You go to driving school and learn to drive a regular-sized car. It takes some practice, of course, but soon enough you'll get the hang of it. Once you know how to drive a car, it's much easier to learn to drive a truck, a lorry, heck, even a bus. While different types of vehicles require different skills, they all have a gas pedal, a brake, and a steering wheel. The basic driving principles apply to them all. You will use your basic car driving skills to drive anything more advanced. The nine habits I am about to present in this book are like learning to drive a regular car. They are the foundation upon which other habits are built—with much more ease. These habits are called keystone habits.[1] The term was first introduced by Charles Duhigg, the author of *The Power of Habit*.

Keystone habits are not easy to adopt; they require commitment, dedication, and practice. I won't lie to you, it will take some time to master them. But once you've nailed them, every other related habit will be much easier to learn.

Let me give you an example, self-discipline. If you work your self-discipline muscle, a lot of good things can come to your life. You'll become more persistent, more resilient, less likely to give up, and more likely to stick to commitments such as doing regular exercise. It is much easier to concentrate your efforts on becoming generally more self-disciplined than to try to maintain productivity at work, forcing yourself on a diet, and becoming a good listener at the same time, right?

Before we delve in the nine keystone habits, let's first ask ...

What are habits?

You probably think that's a funny question to even ask. Of course you know what a habit is! It's something you keep on doing, right? The dictionary definition of habit is "a settled or regular tendency or practice, especially one that is hard to give up." It is something you keep on doing, and you don't even think about it.

There's the key right there. Habits require little to no thinking before you do them. Actually, thoughts do go into your habits, but it all happens in your subconscious. Your habits are an automatic response to the cues that happen throughout your day. Certain situations, people, and things you see on a daily basis elicit a response in your mind that makes the habit happen.

Charles Duhigg in his book *The Power of Habit* talks about numerous studies on how habits are formed and maintained. Based on Duhigg's book, the formation of habits can be broken down into three different parts.[2] An environmental cue leads to a behavioral response, and then a reward.

$$\text{CUE} \to \text{BEHAVIOR} \to \text{REWARD}$$

For example, let's say you bite your nails. Millions of people bite their nails. It is a habit that is extremely hard to get rid of. In fact, there are even substances you can paint onto your nails to make them taste bad in hopes you'll stop biting them. But why do so many people bite their nails? The problem is that people don't fight the right enemy. The enemy is not nail biting itself, but the trigger elicited by a cue that you associate with biting your nails.

This could be your boss calling you into a meeting unexpectedly, a long night of boredom from studying, or maybe your nails just grew a little more and it's time for you to bite them. These cues trigger your mind's desire to perform the behavior. When you start biting your nails, your brain relaxes a little and you feel better by performing the habit.

In order to break this habit or form new habits, you need to focus on the cues instead of the behavior. You need to focus on the boredom from studying, on the sense of meaninglessness another pointless meeting causes. Remind yourself that these things are dull, a pain in the backside, and instead of starting to chew on your delicious nails, take three deep breaths instead. In and out. It will be hard to remember this switch in the beginning. You will make mistakes. However, you'll find yourself breathing more and more often when boredom kicks in. Changing a habit requires a certain amount of mental presence.

Most of us zoom in on the habit itself. For example, you want to start cooking dinner instead of eating out every night. So instead of focusing on just making your dinner, create a routine leading up to cooking dinner. One way to help yourself is to choose an easy cue to start with. Maybe the cue is getting home from work and feeling hungry. Right when you get home from work, focus on the routine that will develop your habit of cooking dinner. Light up a candle, put on an audiobook or relaxation music. Pull out the ingredients you need to cook dinner. If the ingredients are already out by the time you get out of your work clothes and do anything else you need to do, you're going to cook.

Day after day, continue this same routine. You'll notice soon that you don't have to think about going to the fridge and pulling out ingredients—it will just happen. This is your habitual response to your environmental cue of getting home from work.

The reward of cooking the dinner, on one hand, is the delicious and healthy meal that you get to eat once you finish cooking. But on the other hand, you can keep at home some dessert, like your favorite ice cream, to reinforce the target behavior after you've completed it. Home-cooked meals are delicious, and you may find yourself looking forward to getting new recipes and cooking up something new.

When there is something in your life that you want to change, habits can help you get there. The creation of new habits can be applied to your personal life to ensure that you have a better life of your making. Throughout this book, I will outline the different habits that highly successful people have so that you can create a better life.

These new habits will help you change your daily routine and set you up for success. It's a long path to walk, but each day you're taking action, you'll become better than the day before.

Chapter 1

Self-Discipline

Have you ever heard of the marshmallow experiment? It sounds like something I'd definitely want to be a part of. Marshmallows? Yum! On a more serious note, in 1972, psychologist Walter Mischel conducted an experiment with children and marshmallows.

One by one, he called the children in the room where the experiment took place and gave them a single marshmallow. After dispensing the sweets, he said he had to leave for a little while. Before leaving the room, he told the children if they waited until his return to eat the marshmallow, he would give them an additional marshmallow when he got back.

The results were the following: one-third of the children ate the marshmallow right when Mischel left. Another third waited for a little while, but then ate the marshmallow anyway. The last third waited the fifteen minutes it took for Mischel to get back and were rewarded with another marshmallow.

Mischel was interested in seeing if a child's age correlated with their ability to be self-disciplined and delay gratification. Based on his experiment, he concluded that older children could wait longer before eating the marshmallow.

Twenty years after this experiment, Mischel tracked down the now-grown-up children to see if the ones who didn't delay gratification (immediately ate the marshmallow) were less successful than the ones who did delay gratification (waited for Mischel to get back).

Mischel found that the children's ability to delay gratification had a strong connection with their success later in life. The correlation was greater than almost any other measure, including intelligence, test scores, income, religion, personality type, and gender. Psychologists continued to revisit and replicate this study to find that individuals who are able to delay gratification longer were physically healthier, more successful academically, financially more stable, and had a better quality of life.[3]

Even though these findings have been proven time and time again, the ability to delay gratification and hold greater self-discipline seems to be at an all-time low in our society. More people are obese and in debt, consumed by entitlement and anxiety, and our attention spans are shrinking. So what's going on?

Our generation currently focuses on self-esteem rather than self-discipline. And because of this shift of focus, the effects we are experiencing are rather harmful. We need to develop our self-discipline and learn to hone in our focus to create a higher quality of life.

HOW TO BECOME MORE SELF-DISCIPLINED

In order to become more self-disciplined, we need to strengthen a mental muscle. This muscle is willpower, which is not an endless well. In 1998, Roy Baumeister made a discovery in the field of psychology pertaining to willpower.[4] He proved that people who are forced to use their willpower on one task have less willpower to execute upon another task.

In his study, Baumeister placed cookies in front of individuals and told them to resist eating the cookies. After these individuals had to use willpower to resist eating the cookies, they had to perform problem-solving tasks like puzzles. Results showed that the people who resisted eating the cookies did worse on the problem-solving tasks than the individuals who indulged themselves by eating the cookies.

Other psychologists worked to reproduce this data time and time again and found that if you have to exert willpower on one task, you will be less focused and worse at exerting willpower on tasks that come after. This research showed that willpower could be drained.

The phenomenon is frequently referred to as willpower depletion. What do you do after a hard day of work? Are you hyped up on energy and ready to get more stuff done? Doubt it. Most of us just want to sit on the couch, watch some Netflix, and shovel Ben & Jerry's ice cream into our mouths. Willpower depletion is also responsible for why it's easy to convince us to eat a whole pizza or chocolate cake after a week of strict dieting. When we get a lapse in our willpower, it's easier to give in to those temptations.

Thankfully, we can all hit the willpower gym. Think of your willpower as a muscle that can be exercised and made stronger. But because it's like a muscle, it can also be completely neglected. The strength of your willpower is all up to you.

Some things for our willpower get easier as we get older. Remember how hard homework was in elementary school? But hey, once you got to college, homework became second nature. By the time you hit the age of fifty, most boring, dull tasks like paying bills and filling tax reports are as simple as your ABCs. This is because as we age we get more experienced and well practiced in certain activities. We get a higher threshold for willpower depletion.

The same goes for the overachievers you have in your neighborhood. Ever looked at the perfect PTA mom and thought, *how does she do it all?* Or that Mercedes A-class father who has it all together—the job, the family, the appearance? Well, these individuals aren't superhuman or even all that extraordinary. They have simply built up their willpower muscle, or put differently, their fuel tank is bigger than most people's.

Practicing willpower over a long period of time allows those things that started off as hard to become the new normal. If your willpower is feeling a little weak, studies have shown that putting yourself into a positive or competitive mood can restore it.

Listening to your favorite jam can help bring back that willpower. So can glycogen, the result of eating something sweet or starchy.

Don't worry, I won't tell on you for shoving that marshmallow in your mouth. It's only helping your willpower (as long as you weren't told you needed to wait to eat it, of course).

WHY DO DIETS FAIL?

Jumping off the sugar train for a minute, let's talk about dieting. Dieting is something people often do. But just like a certain someone I know, most people fail at their weekly or monthly diet. Why is this?

When someone says they are going to lose ten pounds in three weeks, they are going into the diet with a "crash" mentality. They choose whatever diet they read about that week and then they say, "I won't eat desserts. I'm going to skip my morning breakfast. I will work out for thirty minutes five times a week. I will lose ten pounds. I will be happy."

This becomes their new mantra that they chant as the smell of waffles and Ding Dongs from the vending machines waft over to their desk. Every time they get a whiff of those foods they are constantly saying no to, their willpower takes a hit. After so many punches, willpower gives up.

So what ends up happening? People fail at their diets. They don't hit their goals, and because they focus on this small goal, they do not form any healthy habits. Their ego depletion catches up to them, and pretty soon they are shoving Nutella-covered donuts and KFC down their throats with a side of a sugary drink.

Sure, you can make a few good decisions and practice your willpower for an hour, a day, or even a week. But eventually, your well runs dry and you end up caving to those cravings.

If you do happen to achieve your goal and lose the weight you wanted, there's still a storm on the horizon. Research has shown people who lose weight while dieting end up gaining it back, and then some. Unfortunately, diets bleed from more than one wound.

Diets are the perfect example of why you need to integrate self-discipline as a keystone habit into your daily life to achieve the outcome that you want. Having the willpower to say no to a chocolate chip cookie isn't going to keep you skinny; it's the discipline to choose salad and smoothies that will keep the weight down. You can't rely on willpower only to give up bad-for-you foods; instead, you need to develop new tastes for healthy food.

I talked earlier about changing the cue instead of focusing on your goal itself. *When you change your cues, you give your willpower a break.* No longer does willpower need to run marathon after marathon. Instead, it steps to the sidelines and the real work begins. If you change your cue, you can better reach your ultimate goal.

For example, if work causes you to go to the refrigerator and stress-eat, you should be stocking the refrigerator with healthy food. Take away the chocolate chip cookies and change your cue to grabbing crunchy carrots or sweet strawberries.

Or, even better, when work stresses you out, instead of going to the fridge, get up and do ten jumping jacks, or worse, burpees. Or take a walk around the office building, or do a small meditation session. Developing these new habits will help you stay healthier in the long run.

Most people empty out their willpower cache on a daily

basis, and thus they become less disciplined. You would think that at least the willpower gets spent on worthwhile tasks. Unfortunately not. Your willpower is emptied doing mundane and tedious tasks, in most cases. Developing lifelong habits is a much more worthy cause of draining your willpower.

Have you ever set a New Year's resolution? Maybe you even set a few of them? How many did you fulfill? New Year's goals hardly ever work to our advantage. Most people quit within the first six weeks. Plus, research shows that people who set multiple goals at a time end up accomplishing none of them.

Why? Because they end up burning out. In order to accomplish goals, they need to focus on one goal at a time and slowly build momentum to make that goal happen. Your willpower is only used for new behaviors until they become habitual. *Once a behavior becomes a natural reaction to an impulse, you no longer have to think of it anymore.*

So, if you want to lose ten pounds, focus on creating an environment that will make that goal a reality. Stock your refrigerator with only healthy items, park far away from the store entrances, get a walking treadmill desk, turn off the TV until you exercise for the day, and continue to change your cues so the action of losing ten pounds is inevitable.

EXERCISES TO INCREASE YOUR SELF-DISCIPLINE (AND WILLPOWER)

1. In order to increase your self-discipline and willpower, you need to observe your behavior and note when you are less likely to act in a disciplined way.

2. To know when you're not disciplined, you need to establish what discipline means and looks like for you. Your first task therefore is to write a paragraph on this topic. Start like this: "When I'm disciplined, I ..." and fill the dots with whatever comes to your mind.
3. After you established what your disciplined self looks like, it's time to find the discrepancies between your desire and your current behavior. For the next week don't do anything else but observe your actions and take a note when you act differently than desired. Make sure to include in your note when you acted in an undisciplined way, why you acted that way, and what triggered your undisciplined reaction. Get familiar with your regular responses to stimuli. There is no way of changing something unless you know what to change.
4. After the inventory week is done, read through your notes. Can you see commonalities in your behavior? Any pattern? Any predictability?
5. Make an action plan about the changes you want to implement. For example, if you noticed yourself being hungry in the morning and hopping onto a fast, unhealthy snack to ease your hunger, change the cue. The problem is that your stomach feels empty. Make sure that the first thing you see is something you can fill your stomach with, and that it is healthy. You could put a tall glass of water beside your bed and drink it when you wake up *before* you get out of the bed. This way, you won't feel the urgency to grab the easiest-to-swallow snack, and you may have the willpower to make some scrambled eggs or a granola-yogurt mix.

6. Be consistent with the self-discipline practice of your choice and take a mental note of the change you experience over time. Once you don't feel like your practice is a chore, congratulations! You made a change in your life! It's time to choose something else to work on.

Chapter 2

Take Risks

Before we jump into how to become more comfortable with risks, let's see how people learn to be fearful and avoidant—the main reasons for risk aversion.

We can learn to be fearful in our formative years because of repetitive traumatic events. When as children we are exposed to direct criticism or violence, it can leave deep marks. We don't even have to think about horrific abuse. For example, if someone was often hit when they were late returning home as a child, as an adult, they will be notoriously punctual. If they run late occasionally, they will feel anxious and fear punishment.

Some behaviors of our loved ones can teach us how to be chronically fearful, too. Maybe our parents were always afraid of something, so we were raised in an environment where fear was the main decision-maker. Negative remarks like "We have been farmers for ten generations, only being a farmer is safe." don't seem harmful, but they instill a fixed idea in our mind about what's safe for us to be. If we don't meet expectations and live by the predictions of our parents, we'll feel unsafe.

Extreme traumatic experiences are another way we learn to be afraid. If you fall on the fireplace as a kid, you'll fear fire. If you nearly drown, you'll fear water. If you get stuck somewhere, you'll fear tight spaces. Even thinking about fire, water, or tight spaces can trigger a strong emotional and even physical response.

Lastly, there are fears that we create for ourselves. Self-made discouragements. Sometimes we take on challenges we are destined to fail—for example, people who haven't exercised for half a year sign up for a rim-to-rim hike in the Grand Canyon. In spite of all the warning signs and indication that only the highly fit should embark on the journey, the conclusion the self-sabotager may draw on a helicopter headed to a hospital is to never try hiking again.

People often dive into impossible situations just to have something to complain about, or to justify their lack of motivation and courage. "See, I tried and failed. Now can we all agree this is not for me?"

The fear categories presented above show the insidious ways we learn to be afraid of certain things subconsciously. The result of a fearful mindset is a high level of *risk aversion*.

Risk is directly proportional to the chance of failure. In other words, the more risky something is, the greater the chance for failure. Risks are unpredictable. That's why they are so frightening—because people fear the unknown. We are not fortunetellers. We cannot guess what tomorrow will bring. We hesitate to take action today because we fear the risk of tomorrow. *I won't invest my money. I won't ask that girl for a date.*

But without risk, there is no reward.

FINANCIAL RISK

A quantifiable example is investing money. The higher our risk tolerance, the higher yield we can earn if we invest in certain money-market products. The greatest investors and businesspeople engage in high-risk businesses and they bet successfully more often than not. Even when they fail, they don't get discouraged. They learn the lesson and try a different approach the next time. To them, risk means either victory or a great lesson. Either way, they take away something. Besides, they have a strong knowledge base about the field of investing, they are able to do their own accounting (understand numbers), and they have high risk tolerance.

Knowledge is an antidote to fear of risk. As soon as you have theoretical and practical knowledge, fear of risk will decrease significantly. A lack of knowledge is risky in every field, not just in finances.

SOCIAL RISK

People generally fear rejection just as much as they fear the unknown. Have you ever pretended to agree with your partner when in fact you didn't? Are you often saying things or acting against your values just to please those around you? Do you fear losing the acceptance of others?

If your answer was "yes" to the questions above, then you might fear taking *social risks*. You may live your life based on others' opinions and requirements. You don't want to assume the risk of exposing your own personality because you fear others will ostracize you.

However, you're also frustrated by all those disagreements you didn't express. Your inner peace will be disturbed because you know you feel and think differently. The feelings of desperation and guilt mix in your mind. In the long term, this kind of behavior can result in mental or physical problems.

Accept that you can't satisfy everyone. There will always be people who won't like you, who won't agree with you, but there will be others who do.

EMOTIONAL RISK

The symptoms of the fear of losing your partner are very similar to the previous example, fear of rejection, but here the person you try to please is your significant other or the people closest to you. This is a situation when you don't want to take *emotional risks*.

When two people meet, they try to show their best sides to each other. It is natural to want to be as appealing as possible to someone we feel attracted to. But feeling the need to appear different than who we are can be a sign of low self-confidence. We don't think we'll be loved as we are. Then, as time passes, it is more and more difficult to maintain the false image.

The person close to us notices the difference and becomes

more distant. Or maybe they are in the same boat as we are, struggling to maintain a false image. However, a slow change in behavior is felt, and this is when the fear of loss kicks in. We don't want to lose the other person. We don't understand why they behave differently. So, we start to please them however we can because we think the changes are the harbinger of a breakup. We don't confront; rather, we try to hide how we feel to not risk separation.

The best way to prevent this situation is by not pretending from the start, of course. But if the damage is already done, one can still choose to be honest. Then it is up to the partner if they want to continue the relationship with a clean slate.

If you think you have something to confess and wish to save your relationship, sit down with your partner and tell them about the things you pretended to be and why. Be vulnerable and genuine. Talk about your reasons for pretending to be someone else. They usually involve a low sense of self-worth, a strong fear of being abandoned, and so on. You might add that you'd like to become the person you pretended to be. Once you open up and you allow your partner to see and love the real you, the fear of emotional risk will disappear.

INTELLECTUAL RISK

Fear of confrontation arises when you find yourself in a situation where you have to stand up for yourself and directly confront others.

Let's stick to the example of a verbal confrontation, not a physical one. In a verbal showdown, facts and arguments are the weapons. The winner will be the one who has better arguments. When you engage in such a debate, you take an intellectual risk.

If you face a biology professor, you will probably feel intimidated and afraid to take an intellectual risk, to argue, for example, about the process of photosynthesis. This makes sense. It is not fear, it is common sense.

If you start an argument on a topic where you know you don't have the necessary knowledge, you assume unwanted risk. You'd probably lose the verbal judo, you'd be humiliated, and you'd probably be reluctant to accept a challenge even in your field of expertise. But if you happen to be a biology professor as well, or simply mad about biology and have been reading about it since childhood, you can give it a try. Approach the argument as a listener first, gauge the expertise of the other person, be interested in the other's opinion, and even if it is an argument, try to transform it into an exchange of views.

If possible, avoid engaging in a verbal confrontation even if you're confident of your knowledge on the topic. It is not necessary to show off. Know that you always have a choice. Even if somebody is provoking you to engage in an argument, you can always say, "Yes, this is my opinion about the topic, but I'd be very interested in yours. I might be wrong."

There will always be risks we can either ditch or embrace. Always. It takes courage to engage, to assume risks. You may think you don't have enough courage, but you do. In fact, you are the only one who can limit yourself. Expand your limits.

If you think that people who take the seemingly biggest risk—like poker players and extreme sports practitioners—are just amazingly courageous and badass, you're wrong. They are, rather, nerds, not people with exceptional powers. These people sweat more over figuring out the details of their task than from the task itself. They do their homework and explore the theory of their situation inside out precisely because they have so much to lose. But thanks to the knowledge they gather, the risk actually diminishes.

Big risk-takers aren't waking up, and while drinking their morning coffee, figuring, "Yeah, it would be awesome to take a random risk today." No, not them. Planning, research, and analysis precede the risk-taking.

You can apply this rule to any risk. If it can be applied to big-time investing, why couldn't it be applied to a career change, a request for a raise, or asking your sweetheart to marry you? Know your situation and your objectives. The more you know, the more successfully you can make a decision.

Big risk-takers are often stereotyped as reckless, impulsive people who just hustle through life and get lucky. They are actually planners above everything else. By the moment you see their big risk-taking, they already took dozens and dozens of small risks that led them to the big one. For us it may seem that they are taking an impossible risk, but for them it is just a regular Thursday afternoon. Taking risks became their habit. They worked hard to get where they are now, tested their skills, expanded their boundaries, and overcame their fears to ensure success.

Let's look at a practical example. Have you ever seen a video on YouTube about people do tightrope walking above a giant, impossible abyss? They seem so casual walking up and down, jumping, and balancing themselves. Your blood freezes just by watching it. They didn't just wake up thinking, "Oh yeah, today is a great day to die." Years, maybe decades of work are culminated in the video you are watching. They had the training, the practice, the equipment, and the notion that yes—they can die. But they have done everything humanly possible to prevent it.

Today while browsing on social media, I read two catastrophic news articles. One was about a person who was just walking down the street when something fell on his head, and he died. The parents of the unfortunate boy were devastated as they described their son as hyper-vigilant, never seeking danger, always trying to be safe. The other article was about an acrobatic building climber who made a wrong step on a tall building, fell, and died. Both people met the same unfortunate ending. But do you know what commenters said? Ninety percent of the commenters felt sorry for the unfortunate boy who died by something falling on his head. What do you think ninety percent of people said about the acrobatic climber? "He was asking for it." "He deserved it. Why did he have to climb up there?" I found these comments insensitive and infuriating. I closed my computer on the spot, proving to myself again that spending time on social media is nerve-wracking unless you appreciate the free anthropological lesson you get. Both deaths were tragic. Both deaths were the result of being in the wrong place at the wrong time. Making a bad step. Neither of these people were asking for the end they met—they didn't deserve it. Simply, life sometimes happens and sometimes it ends in quick, senseless ways. You don't need to be an acrobat to die a senseless death. But who lives happier? Someone who has taken the risks and has no regrets or someone who hasn't?

We don't realize that we always take risks—every minute of the day. We don't know when a rock will fall on our head and kill us. We can't prepare for that. Leaving our house is a fifty-fifty chance—either you'll survive the day, or you won't. It is the same chance that you, a pedestrian, and the tightrope walker face. Yes or no. The tightrope walker is actually much more aware and prepared than you are for an accident to befall them. If you want to avoid risk, stay home and make sure there are no pictures hung above your head.

We already are taking a risk by being alive, whether we acknowledge it or not. And this is a short life.

Don't waste it. Overcoming the fear of taking risks is an invaluable habit to have. Don't take big risks first. Just take slightly bigger ones than your comfort zone. Let them lead you to a place where nobody dares go. Then live like nobody does.

Keep in mind: Risk is all about planning and researching, not recklessness.

Even with the best possible preparation, mistakes can happen. Big risk-takers know this very well. If we talk about people putting their lives at risk, they are at peace with any outcome. They know that every jump, every walk, every dive can be their last. They accept the risk and do their best to avoid the worst outcome. They know that failure can happen. They are prepared. They expect failure—a lot of it.

But again, well-prepared risk-takers know their jam inside out; therefore, they can come up with solutions to their failure quicker and more effectively than those who have no clue of what they are doing.

Risk + failure + learning + repeating = growth. This is the equation of practicing taking risks as a keystone habit. Becoming more comfortable with taking risks spills over into many areas of our lives. We'll be more ready and comfortable in saying yes to things we didn't before. The quality of our life will increase thanks to the challenges we dare to undertake, thus growing our self-esteem. People around us will appreciate our guts and find some inspiration in our fearless living.

Chapter 3

Focus

"You don't get results by focusing on results. You get results by focusing on the actions that produce results."

—Mike Hawkins

Think of your focus like a mirror. If the mirror is shattered, it won't show a reflection very well. However, if the mirror is whole, if it is in one piece, it will be able to show the reflection perfectly.

If you create a goal for yourself with divided focus and a shattered mirror, you won't be able to see the whole picture. Your willpower will suffer and decrease during the struggle of figuring out what the next step is. You need to go after what you want with a laser-sharp focus on the next step. Have a clear vision about what you want to do and what you need to do to achieve it.

Cultivating laser-sharp focus is our third keystone habit.

WHY DOES ATTENTION DROP?

Throughout long periods of studying in the conventional education system, I lived for those study breaks. I would step away from the books and take a moment to grab a snack or do just about anything else. If I didn't take study breaks, my mind would wander, and all of a sudden I would catch myself thinking about that embarrassing time I tripped on the bleachers during a sporting event.

It's almost common sense that if you focus on one thing for too long, you find yourself not remembering a lot of it. Also, you will feel distracted or bored. One minute you're reading, and the next you can't remember the last five paragraphs your eyes scanned over. This strange phenomenon was studied by scientists.

Alejandro Lleras, a psychology professor at the University of Illinois, directed a study on a concept known as vigilance decrement.[5] Vigilance decrement is believed to be the decline of a person's performance over time while doing a task. Previous psychologists believed that vigilance decrement occurred because attention is finite and would get used up over time.

Lleras thought differently. He believed that your attention does not just get used up over time. He proposed that poor performance happens because the person is no longer paying attention to their task. One is always paying attention to something, but the task is no longer holding their attention. *It is not the attention itself that is the problem; it is that one's attention is focused elsewhere.*

The human brain adjusts and adapts to a stimulus that

remains constant. For example, think of your friends and how they smell. Maybe you have a friend whose house always smells of cinnamon. But if you asked that friend what her house smelled like, she would probably say it just smells like home. She is used to the scent.

Just like you may not be able to tell what your house smells like, most of us are unaware of our clothes touching our skin. Because we constantly wear clothing (here's hoping), our body adapts to the feeling so that clothing doesn't register in our brains any longer.

Lleras took this knowledge and adapted it into a study to test his hypothesis that vigilance decrement is not from attention being used up, but because your attention is focused on a different stimulus.

One group in Lleras' study performed a fifty-minute task with no breaks or diversions. There was then a switch and no-switch group that had to memorize four different numbers before performing the task. They were later asked about their memory of the numbers at the end of the task. The no-switch group was shown the same numbers given to the switch groups, but were told to ignore them.

As expected, the performance of most of the individuals declined as the task continued on. But the switch groups who took two small breaks from the task stayed focused throughout the experiment and performed better.

Our brains are made to detect and respond to change. When there is change during an activity, our brain performs better because it diverts our attention for a few minutes.

DIGITAL DISTRACTIONS

Social media, your partner, your friends, your Candy Crush app, and countless other things send you notifications. If you have notifications turned on for all of these items, you probably rarely have an hour without your phone buzzing multiple times or your laptop sending out a high-pitched chirp. When your phone buzzes, you can't just leave it there, can you? No way! You have to check it.

How did people live without their laptops, tablets, smart watches, and phones? It seems impossible that the generations before us didn't constantly have the world at their fingertips. While technology is definitely one of the best things that has happened to us, there are some downsides to a world that is digitalized.

Psychologist Larry D. Rosen conducted a study[6] with students who were made to watch a psychology course and then take a test afterward that would be graded. The students were told that they would be receiving text messages from the study coordinators and they needed to respond to the text messages.

One group ended up receiving no text messages, one group received four text messages, and the last group received eight text messages, all within a thirty-minute window. These text messages were sent during important parts of the psychology course that they were to be tested on after. The results found that the group who received four text messages did just fine but the group that received eight text messages suffered on the test.

Rosen and his team did not tell the students when they needed to respond to the text messages, only that they needed to respond. The students that responded immediately to each text message did far worse than the students who waited a few minutes to respond.

The students who waited to respond to the text message were using what is called their *metacognition skills*. Metacognition is the ability to know when your focus is needed and when it may not be.

With insane amounts of digital distractions, many of us struggle with our metacognition skills. Digital distractions lead to broken focus, and it ends up taking us a lot more time to finish a task correctly.

This is especially true in younger generations who have grown up with technology. Even when they are off their phones and computers, thoughts of who may be calling or texting them are surfacing in their minds. Research has found that their focus time is only three minutes. Neurological studies have even shown that individuals who play video games have brain graphs similar to those of addicts. These technological distractions are damaging our focus in the long run.

One way to get back your focus is to take a break from technology. Play a risk-and-reward game. When you work or study for a certain amount of time, reward yourself with your technology for a minute or two. Respond to texts, browse social media, do whatever you want for a few minutes and then get back to work. Start with ten to fifteen minutes and then gradually increase your work time as your focus improves.

If you don't trust your self-restraint or you don't want to deplete your willpower, there are good apps that can help you regulate your access to technology. Fight technology with technology. There is an app for Mac called Self-Control, which can shut you out from sites you don't want to visit for a given period of time. The advantage is you can't get around the program. If you lock yourself out of Facebook for three hours, you're out. Restarting your computer won't overwrite the program. This, however, can be a disadvantage if you want to get something done on a site you locked yourself out from. My advice is to set only one- to two-hour sections of restricted time. You can always restart the hours, and you can save yourself from frustrations that the self-made exclusion might cause.

DOODLING HELPS MAINTAIN FOCUS

My notebooks were always filled with small pictures that I would draw over and over again on the margins, the tops of the page, even sometimes in between the notes I was taking. I did this for almost every lecture or meeting I sat through. My friends would poke fun at me because I would remember everything afterwards, and I got good grades at school and was endorsed by my superiors at work.

They said things like "You must be a really good guesser. All you do is draw!" every time I got a good grade on a test or a shoulder pat at work. Well, I might be a slightly good guesser, but I also focused during classes and meetings. How did I do this? I doodled!

In high school, I even got called out in class one day by one of my favorite professors. He was joking, but he made the comment of, "He gets so bored during my class that all he does is draw!" Basically, he was saying I don't pay attention to his lectures. But it was actually the opposite.

Throughout my doodling, I didn't fall asleep during class, I lost focus less often than my friends, and I got to draw a few cool pictures and make my notes look more exciting.

Research actually backs me up. Before you think about the people always drawing and chewing the tip of their pens during important lectures or business meetings, you might want to take note from those individuals. Doodlers prevail when it comes to focusing and remembering the things that are presented to us.

One study asked a group of individuals to listen to a very long and boring audio clip. Half of the individuals were told to color in different shapes (doodle) and the other half weren't. Both groups had to write down names from the audio clip. The doodlers had to switch between doodling and writing down the names, whereas the other group just had to write down the names.[7]

Guess what happened? Those doodlers remembered a lot more of the names—29% more on average.

The assumption can be made that doodling helps our memory. But how does a small action like doodling help us focus better? One reason may be because we don't daydream while doodling. We are focused on creating the piece of art and our attention is on the paper.

Whether or not you think you are an avid daydreamer, we all do it. Daydreaming uses a lot of the brain's resources. One minute you're listening to your boss conduct a meeting, and the next moment you're thinking of going to Hawaii and what island you want to stay on, what fish you may see snorkeling, and why saying "aloha" sounds so much better than saying "hello."

Daydreaming takes over your executive functions. Doodling, on the other hand, requires little from your executive functions. You are using just enough of your brain to stop daydreaming while you're still listening to what is going on.

The key to doodling is knowing when to practice it. For example, if you are sitting through a long meeting or lecture, doodling can help you stay focused. But if that meeting is showing multiple graphs and reports from your company, doodling is not going to help you.

Doodling helps when your ears need to be active. Doodling does not help when your vision is required. Splitting your visual processing between images and doodling will produce negative results.[8]

If you are feeling overwhelmed or are having trouble processing emotion, doodling may help you there too. Your doodles can help you understand your emotions a little bit more, so you can kill two birds with one stone by processing your emotions and staying focused.

Chapter 4

Lifelong Learning

You know how the saying goes: "You can't teach an old dog new tricks." This means that once you are past a certain age, you can't learn new things. While this may be true in some regards, like how learning a new language gets harder the older you get, learning doesn't stop once the clock strikes midnight on your eighteenth birthday. If it did, we would have an awkwardly chaotic society. Recent brain studies have shown that our brain is capable of learning even in our eighties thanks to a feature called neuroplasticity. This fancy-sounding word means that our brain is capable of reorganizing and growing over time. When we engage in new learning, new pathways and connections are created in the brain.[9] Adopting the simple practice of learning something new daily therefore is an essential keystone habit to keep our brain in shape.

Lifelong learning came from the term "lifelong learners," which was created by Leslie Watkins and used frequently by Professor Clint Taylor (CSULA). The concept says that learning is not confined to formal education in a classroom. Learning happens all throughout your life and happens in many different situations.

Promoting greater and continued learning throughout your adult life is the basis of lifelong learning. It is based on Delors' four pillars of education. Jacques Delors was the eighth president of the European Commission. His four pillars of education for the future are learning to know, learning to do, learning to live together, and learning to be. These four pillars of education encompass what lifelong learning is all about. Lifelong learning is continuing to gain knowledge for personal or professional reasons.

Just because you finish schooling doesn't mean you should stop learning. Delors' four pillars of educations describe the different ways you learn throughout your adult life.[10]

Learning to know is when you master a tool instead of structured knowledge. It's learning to use new technology instead of learning the theory of how computers are made. Learning to do is ensuring people are ready for the work our society will need now and in the future. This includes future innovation and adaptation. It's like how many people have started learning to code. Coding isn't necessarily new, but our society is growing and needs more coders for things like apps and websites.

Learning to live together and with others is all about learning to work with others and resolve conflicts in a peaceful manner. It also encompasses learning and appreciating other cultures, schools of thought, helping out communities, economic resilience, and being individually competent.

The last pillar, learning to be, is obtaining an education that fosters a sense of completeness. This learning is developing your mind and body, sensitivity, appreciating all beauty, and increasing your spirituality.

These different types of learning are not done in a classroom. Lifelong learning is self-directed and is not forced upon anyone. However, it may be the most important learning curve in our life. If you want to have a well-balanced life where you can have something to look forward to, where you can have an "a-ha" or "wow" moment each day, where you want to be more than you were the day before, you need to continue learning.

The most successful world leaders understand that a healthy and well-balanced life is centered on education. Not the "go to school and score As" kind of education, but the self-chosen, unbinding one. Lifelong learning creates active citizens and more competitive individuals. It also makes our communities more sustainable and makes our society more employable.

The importance of education is constantly preached to the younger generations. You need to get your degree, you need to pursue higher education, and so on. What people fail to mention is that going to a university is not the only way to learn and get an education. And certainly not the last milestone in the learning process. There's some value to the education from the School of Hard Knocks. Sure, it doesn't come with a fancy piece of paper detailing a degree, but it gives you life knowledge.

Our education system is outdated. The grounds of today's education system were laid in the '50s and '60s. Books could be filled with the many things that have changed since then—

technologically, socially, and belief-wise. The zeitgeist of 2020 is definitely not the same as that of 1955. The professionals needed today are not the same as a half-century ago. If you want to have a smoother path in life, or you wish one for your children, take into consideration these lines.

Self-education gives you more than just the benefit of keeping stride with the world. Continuing to learn also helps your physical body. Those brain muscles of yours need stimulation or they atrophy. When you continue to learn, your brain cells atrophy slower because there is a constant need for them to be used. The more you know and the more you learn, the stronger your brain connections become. Your brain cells will also work faster. One should continue learning just for the neurological benefits.

BRAIN PLASTICITY

What's your best asset? If you say your hips or your arms, guess again. Those are great assets too, but the puppet master of your hips and arms, the most important asset, is your one and only brain. This organ, which you will never be able to see—hopefully—is your best friend if trained right, and your worst enemy if left to its own devices.

You get through life by riding your brain's coattails. If your brain is slow, you're slow. Everything slows down as your brain slows down. The only way to stop your brain from being slow is to take care of it. Thankfully, your brain just needs intellectual stimulation to continue running.

The best habit you can adopt, as I highlighted at the

beginning of this chapter, is training your brain. The brain registers the training and, as a response, it creates neuropathways where it is stimulated regularly. This process is called neuroplasticity.

Neuroplasticity means that your brain continues to be malleable throughout your life. It has been previously thought that the brain had a critical period of learning, after which it would remain static and unchanged. The critical period of time was believed to happen in childhood. Researchers argued that your brain's circuits were developed as a child and you continued to hold onto those as an adult.

Some of these assumptions are correct. For example, as a child, you learn to walk and talk. That doesn't change very much as you get older, except for an expansion of these skills. These brain circuits will stay fairly static. But researchers argued that neurogenesis would shut down after the critical period of childhood.

Neurogenesis is the process through which the brain produces more brain cells. These new brain cells form when you learn and process new information. Children's brains are constantly in the process of neurogenesis as they expand their knowledge and learn how the world works. But in the late 20th century, researchers started to study whether or not neurogenesis still occurred past childhood.

It turns out, it does. Neurogenesis doesn't stop the minute you hit the drinking age; instead, it continues to occur throughout adult life and far into old age. This regeneration of brain cells in the process of neurogenesis proved that brain plasticity is present in adult life. But, why is this finding so important?

It proves that adults can learn too. Old dogs can learn new tricks, after all. Those adults continue to get smarter and learn new things even as they age.

However, using neuroplasticity to maintain or change the way your brain is wired may not be as easy as you believe. In order to change the way you think, there are certain steps you may need to take to get your brain on the right track.

PRACTICING NEUROPLASTICITY[11]

If you're looking to retrain your brain using neuroplasticity, you need to keep yourself engaged to get your brain ready for change. When you are bored, unfocused, distracted, or doing things with little effort, your brain is hardly engaged. When your brain is disengaged, it's taking the day off.

Our brains are hard-working. They work nonstop without a break. So when we aren't on the move, our brains are relaxing. It's nice to take a break every once in a while, but when we are not alert, our brain is not firing neurotransmitters, and it doesn't remain active.

When our brains are active and firing neurotransmitters, new connections and pathways are made. The more you do something new, repeatedly, for a long period of time, the stronger the connections between the different firing neurons become. Your brain cells interact with each other. When you learn something and enforce the information through repetition, their cooperation grows.

Imagine a group of people singing at different pitches. It may be loud, but it won't sound very good. Now imagine the same group of people singing in perfect pitch with each other. The sound is clearer, stronger, and nicer. This is what happens to your brain cells. When different cells are firing off, it may keep your brain busy, but it is when the same cells interact and coordinate that the strongest connection occurs. This is when neuroplasticity is at its strongest.

To increase your cells' cooperation, you have to learn something interesting to you, something you can focus on, and that you're willing to repeat as often as it takes to ingrain the knowledge.

Why is repetition important? Because when you do something new, your brain only takes note of it if it was successful or important enough to file away and remember. The first time you try to do something new or different, it is a temporary note. Your brain will probably discard it. If you want to make a change stick, you have to repeat this new task every day until your brain accepts it as permanent. How can you know when is this the case? It's easy. Once it takes more effort not to do the action in question than to do it, it means the brain accepted it as the new normal.

An important disclaimer: your brain is constantly creating new pathways depending on the choices you make. Brain plasticity can be a double-edged sword. As you learn, you also forget. And you may also hardwire things in your brain you don't want. Negative, unhealthy actions repeated over time will also trigger brain plasticity. If you take a bad substance repeatedly, over time you become addicted to that substance. Or if you habitually down-talk yourself, you'll end up cultivating an identity of low self-worth. So if you are making a change, try to ensure it is a positive one that will help further your success.

HOW DOES PRACTICING NEUROPLASTICITY RELATE TO LIFELONG LEARNING?

Lifelong learning is the gateway to neuroplasticity. As you learn, neurogenesis occurs and new brain cells form. Depending on what you choose to continue your education in, this will determine the connections your brain creates.

Academic learning like reading books will help expand your base of knowledge, but books are not the only things you should be learning from. You can also benefit from observing your relationships and learning interpersonal skills.

Our human connections are what make us such intelligent creatures. The quality of our relationships can make or break us. If you want to make your relationships better, there are ways to learn from your and others' mistakes. Pay attention to the patterns you find in your relationships. If you find yourself having the same argument with multiple people, the problem is most likely in your communication.

When you detect conflict in a relationship, ask yourself the question, "Why did this argument happen?" While the basis of the argument could have been your partner not doing the laundry, the real root of the argument could be that you feel like a pushover and along the way you enabled your partner to not help you out.

Once you find patterns and the root cause of the conflicts you have in your life, take a deep look at yourself. "I observed that X (feeling like a doormat) is the real reason of my pain.

What did I do to contribute to this? How do I want to be treated instead? What do I need to change to be treated the way I want?" These are hard questions to answer. And it's even harder to follow through with the solutions you come up with. You may have a lot of work to do to establish new boundaries in your relationship and with yourself. Sometimes relationships don't even survive drastic changes such as demanding more respect and setting consequences if the "new rules" are disobeyed. Change is hard for everyone. Sometimes your partner wants a doormat. And when you cease being one, they won't feel happy anymore. The question is, will you be strong enough to ride the waves of change? If you survive the change together, eventually, just like your brain adapts to the new you, your partner's brain will adapt too.

You can also make adjustments about how you see your work. Our job takes up the majority of our adult time. If you are doing something you hate, your mood will reflect that. If you think the answer to this problem is following your passion, I may have bad news for you.

Following your passion is not always the best bet. Cal Newport, the author of the book *So Good They Can't Ignore You*, comes up with an interesting perspective on why following your passion may be ruining your career. He says that when you follow your passion, it can lead to frequent job changes and added anxiety. You feel the need to jump from thing to thing because it suddenly isn't in line with your passion anymore.

Realistically, most passions should remain hobbies. You can love sports or baking, but it may not make the best career choice. A better path may be picking a job you don't hate. It doesn't have to be something you love doing, just something you are not going to dread the moment you open your eyes in the morning.

Settling for work we are okay doing and pouring a lot of hard work into leads to satisfaction over time. The better you get at your job, the more positive feedback you'll get and the more passionate you'll become about it. Strive to master your job. Make yourself more marketable for work by spending your free time developing new skills needed to advance in your chosen career. These new skills should be rare and valuable for society—something people are willing to pay for. Work with individuals you can learn from. If you want to love your job, you need rare and valuable skills that will give you control over what you do. Feeling in control and good about your level of expertise is what leads to happiness and a peace of mind.

To summarize Newport's idea: When you have desirable skills, people will pay you for them because they are worth something. Choose skills that you don't hate and you are willing to learn to master. Developing these skills is another form of lifelong learning that will help your brain's neuroplasticity.

AUTODIDACTICISM

A word that rolls off your tongue almost as well as Mary Poppins's "supercalifragilisticexpialidocious," autodidacticism has its roots in Ancient Greece. Coming from the Greek word "autos" meaning self and "didacticós," or teaching, autodidacticism means teaching yourself new things.

This skill couldn't become "hip" at a better time. If you look toward the future, it is easy to see that many jobs will be replaced by artificial intelligence over the next few decades. If you don't believe me, do a quick Google search and see all the AI that is emerging. If you are still young and looking for a certain career, look to see if AI has made advances in that market. If it has, you may be better off making some changes about your career path. However, if you are already in your career and see your job being replaced by machines, it's time to teach yourself some new tricks.

Knowing how the future will unfold can give you an idea on what skills may be beneficial to learn and which are the skills you shouldn't waste time on. Our world is becoming more and more technology-based. New software and apps are coming out daily to replace old systems, and people we used to need can now be replaced by upcoming technology. But as computers get smarter, there are still some areas that technology can't replace just yet.

Computers cannot replace skills that require creativity, critical thinking, and connection-making. These skills require abstract relations, and computers are not smart or fast enough to relay these like the human brain can.

Chapter 5

The Law of Attraction

I don't mean law of attraction in a *The Secret* (the book by Rhonda Byrne) kind of way, but in the literal sense—how to become more attractive personality-wise.

You may have heard the old belief that life comes easier for pretty people. The most attractive males and females can be seen as the epitome of success. Good salaries, nice families, and all-around great lives. Right?

Wrong. A study from the *Journal of Business and Psychology*[12] found that it's not your looks that will put you at the top of the pay scale. What really matters is how attractive and appealing your personality is. Don't looks and attractiveness go hand in hand? Sometimes, yes. Oftentimes, no.

The study wasn't based on looks only; it factored in health, intelligence, and overall personality. Those who scored high in these three categories were paid higher salaries. And believe it or not, people deemed "very unattractive" in the looks department were still paid higher than the average unattractive person, or an unlikeable attractive person, when they scored high in health, intelligence, and personality.

This study shakes up the belief that pretty people come with a "beauty premium" or that less beautiful people can't hope for a competitive salary. Individuals actually get paid more because they look healthier, are smarter, and bring better assets to a company with their personality. The desirable personalities were more extroverted and less neurotic individuals. This may be because extroverted people tend to make others feel comfortable and at ease, are more fluent in communication, and generally seem more interested in others.

A study conducted by Swami and colleagues in 2010 studied how personality[13] influences a person's attractiveness level. Male participants rated a group of photographs that contained women of varying sizes. While all participants agreed on the most attractive body type, researchers found that when men were given personality traits linked to the women, a wider range of women were suddenly considered attractive.

The research doesn't stop there. Lewandowski, Aron, and Gee's research also supports the idea that personality influences attractiveness. Photos of both males and females were linked with positive and negative personality traits. The study found that negative personality traits made a person less attractive while positive personality traits made a person more attractive. Also, Paunonen found that a person's perceived honesty is factored into how attractive they are. And finally, talent, efforts, and how well-liked one is in general also influences how attractive one comes across to others.

Attractive, it turns out, means much more than looking like

a Victoria's Secret model or The Rock. If one has a personality that others deem attractive, they too can benefit from the "beauty premium." While cultivating an attractive personality is a seemingly superficial keystone habit, it can help in a lot of life areas, from having better personal relationships, to work relationships, to success in general.

HOW CAN WE DEVELOP AN ATTRACTIVE PERSONALITY?

Thankfully, there are helpful things we can do to raise our standing with our loved ones, coworkers, and peers. Dale Carnegie has some great tips in his book *How to Win Friends and Influence People* on how to become more attractive.[14]

One of his first tips is to observe how we speak to others. Imagine you are a kindergarten teacher. When a five-year-old student of yours colors outside the lines on a coloring page, do you immediately call them out? If your answer was yes, you may come across as cruel. You would probably say something like, "Wow, that's a very pretty picture! Keep coloring."

We have no problem giving constant encouragement to children, who do a million things "wrong" daily. Sure, they are still learning, but guess what? So are adults. When a peer of yours does something you deem "wrong," don't rush to criticize or condemn them. Do you do this frequently? Most of us do. Nothing positive comes from criticizing others. If they accept your criticism, they'll still feel bitter and resentful at heart. If they become defensive, you can end up having a fight for often no good reason.

Carnegie also talks about the desire we all have to feel important in life and how this desire goes unfulfilled. Another way to be more attractive is to make others feel important with an honest and sincere appreciation for what they do. Saying thank you and being appreciative often seems like a given; it's something everyone values so much. Yet we as a society largely struggle with it. When you appreciate others, you become more likable to them. Don't hesitate to express your appreciation when someone does something well.

One day, I was arguing with my wife about some issue we all seem to argue about—the dishes. Let's be honest, many of us hate cleaning. I felt like my wife wasn't helping me out, and I just needed her to do the dishes a few times a week when I was working late. I felt I wasn't asking for much.

On the other hand, my wife thought I was asking way too much. She worked all day too, did a few things around the house, and the second she sat down, I asked her to help with the dishes. I didn't feel I instantly asked her, but she felt so.

We eventually agreed to disagree until two months later, when the argument was brought up again. We were joking about it, but I put my foot down and said, "I'm sure we can both agree now that I was right."

A horrified face met mine and soon I was being told, "Absolutely not! I was right!" And the argument continued. This happens ninety percent of the time. Refusing to listen to and understand someone just makes them stick to their guns even more. If you want to come across as attractive and likable, try to empathize with them. Put yourself in their shoes and see why it makes sense to them to do what they do. Telling someone they are wrong will instantly make them defensive. They will take a hard stance and protect it, even if they are wrong. Many times, no one is wrong or right—you just have different perspectives on the same problem.

Carnegie says, "The average person is more interested in his or her own name than all the other names on Earth put together." Tip number four to be more attractive? Learn (and use) your peer's name, frequently.

If you struggle with remembering others' names, try associating them with something familiar. Like Paula Pepper, or William Water. It sounds silly, but it can help you learn peoples' names quickly. This small compliment will help you stand out from the crowd by making the other person stand out from a nameless crowd.

When we get introduced to someone, usually we are so preoccupied with pronouncing our names correctly and making that handshake as cool as possible that we lose focus on catching the other party's name. If this happens, make sure to ask their name again on the spot. "I'm sorry, I'm not sure I heard your name correctly." This way the person you just met will feel you're truly interested. Make sure to memorize their name the second time.

Strive to be a good listener in general. Everyone had that friend growing up whom they could call and vent their problems to. You didn't call the friend who was always comparing their situation to yours or overpowering the phone call; you went to the one who listened well.

Those who listen attentively are attractive to others. People like to talk about themselves. If you become the listener and encourage others to talk about their lives, it makes them get those warm and fuzzy feelings inside. Try to listen to seventy-five percent of the conversation and talk the other twenty-five. This helps the other person feel important and valued.

Human nature craves the feeling of importance, and it is often this desire that leads us to the next roadblock on the journey to attractiveness: pride. Everyone has experience with pride, but no one wants to admit that they are prideful. Probably for good reason, because prideful people are hard to like.

Your attractiveness can increase greatly if you develop the ability to swallow your pride and admit when you are wrong. You are not wrong all the time, but when you catch yourself being in the wrong, recognize it quickly and admit it to the other person. You may have to eat crow a few times. Admitting fault is not shameful. Being in the place of vulnerability, saying, "I'm sorry, I was wrong," is strength.

Maybe one of the most difficult things some people struggle with is stepping into another person's shoes and trying to see their point of view. It is so easy to dismiss the other. "No, this is how it should be." Remember, there are many paths up the mountain. There are multiple directions to arrive to the same place, and neither is worse than the other. I might crack my eggs, stir them, then put them in the pan and cook them to scramble. You may crack your eggs straight into the pan and scramble and cook them at the same time. We will both end up with scrambled eggs.

Just because someone thinks differently than you does not mean they are wrong. Having an attractive personality means that you can appreciate and try to understand where another person is coming from. This is their journey, not yours. If they wanted your opinion every step of the way, they would've hired you as their guide.

Don't give people a bad rep. They may try to live up to it. If you tell a child they are bad, they are going to think they are bad and often misbehave. The same goes for adults. Give people a good reputation to live up to. If you tell your wife she's lazy and does nothing all day, she won't be motivated to be anything more. If, however, you tell her that you know how hard-working she is and forgetting to wash the dishes was just a one-time thing, she'll feel responsible to live up to your good opinion. She won't forget to wash the dishes again.

Chapter 6

Mindfulness

When you close your eyes and try to think about nothing, what happens? Besides the obvious failure of being unable to think about nothing, your mind keeps thinking. Then you catch yourself thinking and you may let out a frustrated sigh.

Turns out, thinking about nothing isn't truly possible. Your mind still watches your mind. There's a concept in Zen that refers to these two minds as the "thinking mind" and the "observing mind."

Our thinking mind controls much of what we do. People often say that they were "lost in their thoughts." This happens because the thinking mind really does have a mind of its own. Maybe you think you have a really special mind and can control your thoughts. Let's test that thesis.

Whatever you do, do not think about an apple pie. Don't imagine the sweetness of the apple pie as it melts in your mouth. And especially don't think about how much you wish you had it.

You thought about the apple pie. But not only did you think about it, you also watched yourself think about the pie while reading those sentences. Your observing mind was watching your thinking mind and telling it not to think about the apple pie. And yet your observing mind watched as the thinking mind disobeyed. The thoughts of a fresh, warm, cinnamon-scented apple pie entered into your mind.

When thoughts are running through your head like an anxious mouse, your thinking mind is at work. The thinking mind doesn't like to take breaks; it wants action. If it gets obsessed with watching all the seasons of *House of Cards* in a week, or baking a Sachertorte at midnight, your observing mind can't really do anything about it. To avoid inner conflict, the observing mind rather retreats to a peaceful hill, sipping oolong tea, watching as the disobedient, child-like thinking mind runs wild.

Negative emotions can't be repressed because the thinking mind can't be tamed. They are going to continue to pop up automatically. The observing mind, however, can help you prevent overwhelm caused by negative emotions.

Stop for a moment, and as an outsider, take a mental note about what you're feeling. Instead of saying, "I am angry," try saying, "I feel anger." It seems like a little difference, but it helps you to not identify with the emotion. If you have anger, it means you aren't controlled by it. You are not angry, you are not the anger itself—you just feel it, so you can let go of it.

Your emotions are not a choice. But the reaction you have to emotions is within your control. Your reaction is the variable in the equation. For example, sometimes when I sit down to write, anxiety starts to invade my mind. No one wants to read something boring, right? My thinking mind gives me reasons why I shouldn't write like, "No one will want to read this," or, "You're wasting your time." I have these worries but I choose to keep writing despite them.

Negative emotions and excuses never go away for good, even if you handle them well once or twice. They will keep coming back in different shapes and forms, triggered by various events. Negative thoughts and emotions are a part of life; no matter how many methods you use to try to get rid of them. They are natural—sometimes even useful—parts of humanity. The best you can do to your mental well-being is stop fighting emotions. Try embracing, acknowledging, and gently letting them go instead.

As the Buddhist saying goes, "What you resist will persist." The more you fight your negative emotions, the quicker you sink into the mud. Accept your emotions and release them.

I often run into the question, "How do you deal with your fears? How do you handle your fear of being rejected, criticized, or made fun of?" Some of my friends think undeservedly highly of my anxiety management.

In reality, I have the same worries and fears like everyone else. But I make a conscious effort to not identify with them. I accept that I'm feeling fear at the moment, and do whatever I planned to do together with them. Or despite them. I practice to release the control of my thinking mind. I notice what I feel. For example, when I feel my writing-related anxieties, I take a minute to tell myself, "Today I feel anxiety because of writing." Should I not write? Would I ever finish writing a book if I didn't write when fearful thoughts crawled into my mind?

We perceive events according to our own thoughts. When you get into an argument with a partner or friend, your perspectives are probably completely different. We get so caught up in our own brain that when another person says, "That's not how it happened," we immediately jump to defend what we think happened. In reality, the other person may be right. Where is the evidence to support our thoughts? Is this thought process helping you? Blindly trusting our own thoughts can create a slippery slope that leads us into arguments.

The thoughts we have then lead to our feelings, behaviors, and outcomes. If you are constantly thinking poorly about yourself, your behaviors and outcomes will be negative, which then reinforces your negative thoughts about yourself. It's a horrible reinforcing loop to get caught up in. This is why it is vital to keep observing and monitoring our everyday thoughts. If we catch ourselves having a discouraging self-talk, we can choose to change it. Everyone wants to have a happy life—whatever that means. Your thoughts create your reality. If you let dark thoughts overrun your mind, the chances for good experiences exponentially decrease as time passes. The deeper you get into the negativity spiral, the harder it will be to get out.

HOW TO GET A HOLD ON YOUR THINKING MIND

Remember that the thinking mind is rash, like a child. It needs to be nurtured and parented by the observing mind. If a child came up to you and said something hurtful, you would probably brush it off because they're just a child. Your thinking mind is very much like this.

Take your thinking mind's thoughts with a little more than a grain of salt. Not all of your thoughts should be questioned. Most of them help creativity, productivity, and survival. For example, if you think you shouldn't drive through a flooded area or wildfire, or enter in the cage of a hungry tiger, you're right. But thoughts related to concepts such as life, yourself, and human relationships need to be questioned and redefined occasionally. If a negative, painful thought comes up, instead of fighting it, ask yourself, "Where did this thought come from? Is there any evidence to support this actually happening?"

Observing and questioning your thoughts is a lifelong project and a keystone habit. Your mind is your most important asset, and I would like to add another keystone habit besides self-observation and mindfulness. In the next chapter, I'll talk about how you can develop a healthy meditation program and learn to calm your mind while opening up your gratitude.

Chapter 7
Meditation

How often do you meditate? A lot of different news sources and books focus on how meditation can improve our quality of life, yet we do not take advantage of it. While it may seem that meditation is a small habit we harvest from a keystone habit, actually, the opposite is true. Many good habits come easier to us if we meditate regularly.

A recent paper in the journal *Psychological Science* talks about the different brain functions that are improved by meditation. They found that intensive meditation increases a person's focus, even if they are doing boring tasks.

The study was led by Katherine MacLean from UC Davis.[15] Like most psychological studies, it included a boring test. I mean it, this test really was boring. A series of lines would flash on a computer screen. When the individuals sensed that a line was shorter than the rest of the sequence, they would click the screen.

The purpose of the test was to make the participants focus intently even though it was boring. The individuals who meditated were more likely to notice when a line was a different size in the sequence, but they did not react any faster than the control group. So while meditation helps your brain focus and do something automatically, like process visual stimuli, meditation does not help you do things more complicated, like react more quickly. However, the results of this test are still very notable.

Oftentimes, our days are painfully monotonous. Meditation can help us stay alert and focused when our day gets dull, too. While meditation is often considered a more spiritual practice, its effects are well-documented and studied by scientists. Studies have charted how well the brain reacts to meditation.

One benefit of meditation is that it increases focus; in other words, it aids another keystone habit. When you regularly practice meditation, it's easier to focus for longer periods of time on specific tasks. Your mind is better compartmentalized and won't wander as much as before. For individuals who struggle with lack of focus (like many of us do), meditation can be a great catalyst.

You know what all of us could use a little less of? Stress and worry. We as a society are always stressed. What if I told you that in just a few minutes a day, your stress level could decrease? Well, no surprise here, meditation can do that for you. Meditation has been prescribed far longer than any medicine on the market. If you are stressed out, meditation can produce great results in decreasing stress levels.

Another reason to consider doing meditation is to increase

your intuition. You know that gut feeling you get? That's your intuition. Meditation helps you to understand your unconscious and decision-making processes. It increases your self-awareness, and your gut feeling is usually a pretty good judge.

I am a work in progress at remembering things. If I don't have a thousand reminders, I'm pretty much doomed. The first reason meditation started to appeal to me was the proven fact that it helps improve memory. By meditating, I was able to slowly get rid of the clutter in my mind. The things I didn't need to remember flew away and cleared space for the things I did need to remember, like my deadlines.

Our society loves external validation. Between counting our social media likes and seeking others' approval, we can hardly get through a whole day without looking for some compliment or reassurance. Meditation helps us notice and tame these behaviors. You become more aware of your thoughts to recognize when you're being too clingy on someone else.

Meditation won't be the panacea and cure all your problems. But it can help you delve deeper into your subconscious and learn more about yourself. It increases your attention and awareness while sharpening your focus.

If you're automatically dismissing this chapter because you think you cannot meditate, stop right there. There are different ways you can meditate, even if you have a mind that runs a thousand miles an hour. Let's take a closer look at some meditation practices.

HOW DO I MEDITATE?

There are plenty of different styles and techniques for meditating. Meditation is flexible, and one style isn't better than the other; they are simply different. What may work for one person may not work for another. The key to a successful meditation practice is trying out different forms until you find one that works for you.

Meditation includes anything that helps you focus your mind on the present moment, to notice and let go of the thoughts and emotions that arise. For some, this may involve mantras, yoga, or chanting, while for others, this may involve rhythmic walking or counting breaths.

If you are a newbie to meditation, let me share the simplest way to start your new habit. Try sitting and counting your breaths. It's easy to acclimate to and doesn't require you to learn anything new or different.

To start your meditation practice, set aside ten to fifteen minutes of your time. Everyone should have this amount of minutes throughout the day. Set a clock or alarm on your phone to alert you when these few minutes are done so that you are not tempted to get up and check the clock.

Go into a room where you will have no distractions. Grab the comfiest pillow you own and set it on the floor. Sit cross-legged on top of the pillow and make sure your back is straight (no one needs to throw out their back from meditating).

Relax, let your stomach hang out, and look straight ahead. Don't worry, no one is going to be looking at you. You can choose to close your eyes or keep them open, whichever is preferable to you. Put your hands wherever it feels most comfortable.

Now it's time to clear your mind. Focus your attention on your breath; notice as you inhale and exhale. Whenever a thought pops up, just gently tell yourself, "Thinking," and move your focus back to the breath. This is probably going to be challenging the first few times you meditate. Thankfully, it really does get easier. When a thought arises, do not dwell on it. Acknowledge it and let it float away.

You will want to breathe through your nose and expand your belly. If it helps, count each breath, try to get to ten. If you want, you can start your count over each time a thought distracts you, but you don't have to.

Perhaps the most important part of this meditation process is letting go of self-judgment. The practice is noticing the arising thoughts and redirecting your attention to the breath, not achieving thoughtlessness.

The first few times you practice, fifteen minutes is going to seem like a long time. I promise time does not move slower while you meditate, no matter how firmly you believe this. When you do complete a session of meditation, take a note about how you feel. Do you feel more calm and at ease?

Try this simple form of Zen meditation a few times. You can start with ten minutes and slowly add more time as you build up your focus. But if after a few times you think this method is not for you, try a different meditation method.

Even just changing your sitting posture can be a huge help. Try sitting in the seiza pose. Seiza comes from Japanese culture, and it involves sitting with your knees together, your back straight, and your booty resting on those ankles of yours.

If you have bad knees, seiza is going to be difficult, so you'll want to skip this one. But if you try it and like it, it's not going to harm anything.

Half lotus is another pose you can try if you're feeling a little next level. Put your left foot up onto your right thigh and then tuck your right leg under. If you meditate for longer than fifteen minutes, alternate which leg goes on top halfway through your session.

Full lotus is the ultimate flexibility pose. It's what you see in most photos when you look up meditation. In this pose, each foot is placed on the top of the other thigh. If it's easy, great. But if you're struggling with it, don't force it. You can easily injure your knees. Trying all of these poses should be done with the knowledge that they can injure you if you are not prepared physically.

If no sitting meditation works for you, try walking meditation. Get in tune with your body. Observe how your feet lift from the ground, how your weight shifts as you take each step. Involve your senses. Pay attention to the texture of the ground, the sun, the wind. What smells can you detect? What sights are in front of you? Can you distinguish four different noises? Is it cold or warm outside? Just notice your surroundings and your body as a whole.

It doesn't matter how you meditate. It doesn't matter much if you feel a difference afterwards. Your mind will know the difference.

FORGIVENESS

When I was a teenager, my favorite dramatic line was, "I'll never forgive you!" Often said to my parents, I was over it in just a few minutes. I said this in the heat of the moment because I was annoyed and frustrated. And after a few minutes, I forgave them and decided to move on. Why? Because I was so tired ruminating about my misery.

When you hold a grudge against someone, it takes a lot of your time and energy. It's like walking around with a chain. When we let go of this extra weight, we can walk freely.

When something really hurts us, it is hard to forgive. Many of us have experienced how badly a betrayal from someone we love can damage our trust and make us never want to forgive them. This is a normal human reaction and there is no need to beat yourself up if you think you can't forgive someone just yet. When you suffer a betrayal, you might think that forgiving and moving on equals losing. You may feel entitled to your misery—you suffered for it, after all. You invested a lot of time and emotions in this mess. You can't give up on it now.

You might think that by holding on to this anger that you are winning; by staying mad you are punishing the person who hurt you. Really, you are only punishing yourself. As the saying goes, "Anger is like drinking poison and expecting the other person to die."

Forgiveness is selfish. When you forgive someone, you are not condoning their action and blessing them—you're doing it for yourself so that you can feel better.

Most people aren't trying to hurt you. Most individuals

don't go out of their way to try and make you suffer. When you get hurt, it's often because the other person was ignorant in what they were doing. This might be hard to hear. It may be more beneficial to you to believe that the person really was trying to hurt you.

In reality, they just don't know better. When someone hurts you, try to remember your own faults and instances where you made similar mistakes. I've always liked the saying, "Everybody is somebody's monster." It shows that everyone is painted in a bad light according to someone else's perspective.

We all make mistakes. When you learn that others' mistakes are not necessarily more intentional than your own, it's much easier to forgive. Peace of mind is a lot harder to achieve when you are being weighed down by a grudge.

Sometimes people are not even aware they hurt you. You might get worked up and pout for days, weeks, or years while the subject of your anger doesn't even have the slightest clue that they hurt you. If you feel hurt, ask yourself why it affects you the way it does. When you are not emotionally overheated anymore, you can tell the hurtful person, "Look, what you did or said made me feel (…). I assume you didn't want to hurt me intentionally, but you did. In the future I need you to (…)." Tell them exactly what you would like them to change and how the situation can be improved so they can do better in the future.

Speaking about your problems and solving them shortly after the event can cut short a lot of time spent with unhealthy resentment.

GRATITUDE

Why is it so hard for us to be grateful? If you are reading this book, it means you have more than millions of other people in the world. Seriously, you do. You have a Kindle eReader—or a computer, at the very least. You can read! You have access to the Internet, you have a credit card …

The next time you want to complain about something, think about others who never get the chance to experience that. Are you mad that your water has no ice? There are people who never get the chance to drink clean water. Angry that the Internet is slow? Millions of people will never touch a computer.

Life is so much better now than it was even a few generations ago in the Western world. You get to choose who you date, who you marry, when you want to have children, if you want to have children, and a multitude of other things.

Even the poorest of people in America are better off than others in this world. If you live today, it means you are incredibly blessed.

Gratitude has actually been linked to an abundance of health benefits and a happier life.

Learn to appreciate what you have and create a mindset of having enough. When you start to feel envious of others, look at yourself and what you have. Write in a gratitude journal daily. Just jot a few things down in your phone or on a sheet of paper.

Even simple things like, "I'm thankful for clean water, my job, and my dog Fido," will help you become more fulfilled. While it isn't bad to want more, appreciating what you already have helps you feel at peace.

Chapter 8

Have Something to Wake Up For

Do you want to be a millionaire? Maybe you just want greater financial and personal success. If you have an idea of what you want, you need an action plan that lines up with it. If you have a goal without a plan, it's really just a dream. But most importantly, have a goal that keeps you going all the time. It can be a small goal like losing five pounds, or an insane goal like becoming the next governor of California. The keystone habit here is to have something that keeps you excited and, ultimately, alive. Of course, the optimal track to set goals is to start small and build up the ambition over time.

Professor Gail Matthews confirmed the power of writing down goals in a study not long ago. When people wrote down their goals, they were forty-two percent more likely to achieve them. Writing down your goals brings clarity and declares your purpose. It is a level of intention that gives your mind direction, and you can take action even when you are not completely fired up by the goal. Matthews also found that sharing your goal with friends can improve your progress. The reason is that it holds you accountable.

Another study, however, concluded that talking about goals makes them less likely to happen. Why? Because by talking about the goal, you already experienced the positive feelings related to them. Your soul's cravings were satisfied; therefore you may be less likely to take action.

Test yourself on which of the research results describe you more. Are you a person who is more likely to finish a goal just because he said it to someone and wants to stick to his word, or are you less likely to actually take action once you've talked about it? Take a mental note about your reaction and talk or don't talk about your goals with your friends based on your own results.

You need to make sure that your environment will be conducive to the goals you have set. If you want to lose weight, hanging out in a donut shop with your friends doesn't sound like a good idea. But if you want to lose weight and hang out in a gym, your goal suddenly looks a lot more feasible. It would be a lot easier to work out when you are at the gym than it would be to drive to a store and pick up a candy bar.

What you surround yourself with has the ability to make or break your goals. Do you spend a lot of time on your phone? Put it out of sight so you can find better things to do. If your phone is constantly near you, it's easy to pick it up and start searching through social media networks.

Your goals would benefit from removed distractions. For example, if you have a TV in your bedroom, remove it. Place books on your bedside table instead. When you get ready to go to sleep, instead of turning on the TV, turn to a book and read. It becomes a lot easier to read when it is the only option.

If you want to become more financially stable, create a strong budget. Use cash for each budget category. Once the cash is gone, you're done with that category for the month. Creating this environment forces you to stick to a budget rather than rack up charges on a credit card and only check the bill when it's time to pay.

Start by setting small, achievable goals.

Think of yourself training ten dogs at once. What does this picture look like? Complete and utter chaos. Sure, dogs are wonderful creatures, but you can't handle ten of them at once.

Now, picture yourself training one dog. What does this picture look like? Probably a lot calmer and more manageable, with more achievable prospects. It is much easier to train one dog at the time than it would be to train ten. The same goes for your goals. You work better with one, smaller task. The end goal can be to have ten well-trained dogs, but you can better train one dog at a time.

A study conducted by Dan Ariely and his colleagues looked at students who gave themselves strict deadlines compared to other students who didn't give themselves any deadlines. The students who had strict deadlines got much more done and performed better than the students with no deadlines.

However, the students who set generous deadlines performed the same as the students with no deadlines. If you are too easy on yourself with your deadlines and you give yourself too much time to complete a task, your efficiency will decrease almost as much as it would for someone without any clue or restraint. As Parkinson's Law says, "Work expands so as to fill the time available for its completion." What you think you need a month for often can be finished in a week. If you have a month as a deadline, you still do your task in a week after procrastinating for three weeks.

One day, my wife asked me to help her hang the curtains. When I asked her when she needed it done by, she said whenever I could make it work. Well, life was busy, and the next day I didn't get back to her about the curtains. I figured she was waiting for me and she'd let me know if the matter was urgent, so I didn't bother asking about the issue.

Days went by, and one night when I arrived home, the curtains were hung. When I asked my wife how she could manage hanging the heavy beasts, she laughed and told me she had gotten our neighbor to help her hang the curtains. I felt terrible, as a man and as a husband, but I learned my lesson. Helping my wife would have taken twenty minutes out of my day. Because I never set a deadline for hanging the curtains, it just didn't happen. The next time my wife needed help, I set a specific deadline to help her so I wouldn't run into the same issue.

If you want to work efficiently, you need deadlines and to manage your own time. People just procrastinate through tasks sometimes and nothing gets done. Adulthood starts where you can make responsible decisions for yourself—this includes time management.

Take, for example, wedding planning. If a bride tried to plan a wedding in a week, the outcome would be chaotic. That's why brides take a long time to plan their wedding, creating small goals over a long period of time: they find a dress, pick out flowers, choose wedding colors, pick bridesmaids, find a venue, etc. I know, ladies, it is not that difficult—you have everything sorted out on Pinterest five years in advance. My sixteen-year-old lectured me about this the other day. She showed me her "Wedding with Channing Tatum" board on Pinterest. Who is this Channing Tatum? And what should I think about all this as a father?

HOW TO SET A SMART GOAL

SMART goals are specific, measurable, attainable, relevant, and timely. This acronym is frequently used in the professional world. When your goals are SMART, you are much more likely to achieve them.

Imagine you set a goal to lose weight. When? How? If your goal is simply "lose a few pounds," it's not going to happen.

However, if your goal is to fit into your old jeans you partied through your twenties in—"I'm going to lose five pounds by the end of October this year"—you have a specific goal that is easily measured and has a deadline.

When you set a SMART goal, you hone your focus and give yourself what you need to make the goal a reality.

Your goal should be specific. Specific goals ask who, what, when, where, how, and why. When you set your goal to be measurable, it needs to have a set amount, something you can track and check off when it is achieved. Attainable and timely go hand in hand. Relevant means that your goal has to feel like a priority in your life. If you vaguely aim for something you really don't care about, then your chances of success are low.

You can't set a goal like, "I will save $100,000 dollars by March 31st next year," if your yearly salary is only $60,000. Set goals that you know you will be able to take the steps to make them happen. But don't set a goal like, "I will save $200 by March 31st next year," if you could easily put $200 into your bank account weekly.

There is an optimal balance in goal-setting. You need to create goals that will challenge you, but are realistic enough that you know you can make them happen. Here is what your SMART weight loss goal would look like:

- S for specific: Fitting into your old jeans.
- M for measurable: You need to lose about five pounds to fit into those jeans.
- A for achievable: Since it is the middle of August as I write this, losing a pound every two weeks is an achievable target. It is not a sudden, torturous weight loss, but it is not so easy, either.
- R for relevant: You want to feel and look like in your twenties; you want to feel better about your body.
- T for timely: By the end of October this year.

Once you have set your SMART goals, remember to write them down as I did above. Keep the notes about your goals close to yourself so you can see and recall them as often as you need.

Chapter 9

Saving and Budgeting

When I was fifteen, I was very excited to make my own laundry detergent. It was going to save me tons of money a year. All hyped up, I went to the grocery store, bought my borax, baking soda, washing soda, and soap. Got home, mixed up the ingredients, and checked the time. I'd wasted two hours.

"But I saved money!" I thought. Not really. The two hours of my time was worth more than the few dollars I saved by making my own laundry detergent. While some tricks and "hacks" may save you some money, they don't always value your time and energy.

When people want to save money, usually they adopt a scarcity mindset. They cut costs on daily items to the point of being uncomfortable. People try to save a ridiculously small amount of money at the cost of precious time. For example, you walk to a store miles away just to buy a Nutella jar one dollar cheaper. True, you saved a dollar and burned some calories in advance, but you also lost an hour. It means you "paid yourself" with a one-dollar-per-hour wage. Would you work for that?

Some people tend to tie their self-worth to their net worth. They don't take monetary risks because they are afraid of failure. If they grow the guts and still try "making it," but don't get rich on their first try, or lose what little money they have, their self-esteem tank goes totally empty. So does their courage to take any financial risk in this life or the next.

I hear you. You don't have so much money to afford the luxury of self-esteem building or other nonsense. You must pay the bills. I know. I've been there, and I know how crippling scarcity can be. In many cases, you can't change your wallet to meet your needs as quickly as you can change something else: your mindset. Our last keystone habit is working on developing a growth mindset.

What do you think a growth mindset is? Do you think it is about believing strongly enough that you can become rich? Do you think if you concentrate enough and you channel all the power in the universe by your positive thoughts while meditating in a cave, you'll be willing money into your account?

If you roll your eyes and sigh, you're right. Things unfortunately don't work that way. One can't transfer money with the power of thoughts. Unless they are a Jedi. But Jedi don't care about material stuff, so ... there is no way around it.

You can't think money into your account, but your thoughts do play an important role in your finances. The way you think about yourself, of how much you can handle or change, what you think you need, and what you can't live without, all affect the way you handle money.

The conventional thought of, "What the mind can conceive, it can achieve," needs to be interpreted more like, "Develop the habit of thinking that you can learn, improve, and change, and become wealthier as a result."

This is what I think a growth mindset is. A growth mindset is about getting into a habit of learning and developing new skills. It's recognizing that we don't have to feel limited by our current situation in life. We possess the ability to change our circumstances. We can learn and improve despite the situations we find ourselves in.

A growth mindset is also learning to appreciate what we have. The moment we shift our focus from what we lack to what we own, our life won't seem so empty.

You feel that you don't have the willpower to be grateful and positive all the time? No one does. So don't aim for an imaginary target you'll never hit. You can consciously observe the cue that leads you to limiting thoughts and habits. You don't have to be self-loathing to limit yourself. Whenever you avoid a semi-difficult challenge or point fingers at others for your failure, or you compare yourself to others, these are all limiting thoughts.

"I'm going to mess up!"

"It's the government!"

"It's easy to say that if you are rich like her …"

"I never had the opportunity …"

There are many limiting thoughts in your head you actually consider reasonable. Sure, they are true. It is not a lie that you had fewer resources than the kids of Bill Gates when growing up. So what? What can you do about it? Will your situation improve by sulking on the couch about your misfortunes?

If you want more in life, your only option is to persist despite the odds. You think you can't do it?

Switch this thought. Think, "I'll do my best without hoping for anything. I'll see what happens. If I succeed, hurray. If I fail, it will teach me something."

You think others are more gifted and have more resources than you do? Look at these people, learn their tactics, observe what they do better. Apply what they do to your own life. You may realize that you couldn't or wouldn't pay the price they are paying for their success. Relieve yourself of envy.

Resist blaming others for your failures. The key to adulthood is the ability to take responsibility for our actions. You messed up? So what? It happens. Learn your lessons, use those napkins, and move on to do better next time. Do you find it silly or insulting when someone else blames you for something that wasn't your fault? Why would you do the same? Take responsibility for your decisions and actions.

Blaming others is like being angry with your spouse for buying you a donut. It's your choice to eat the donut. Health and financial decisions we make share some similarities. Usually we know what we need to do to be healthier, but we resist doing it until we wake up in a hospital. The same applies to money. We know we should and could manage it better, but we don't do anything until the debt collector destroys our TV with a lightsaber.

Some think the solution is strengthening willpower. By this point, we know that willpower is finite. Instead of depending on willpower only, help yourself by creating systems you can think in to alleviate the burden on your willpower.

A systems-based mindset can help when your willpower fails. Take yourself out of the equation so your willpower is not relied on so much. For example, if you want to save money, make it automatic. Have a certain amount come out of your check each paycheck that you never see. If you don't have to physically transfer the money, it becomes a lot easier to save. With so many apps and resources available today, relying on systems is easier than ever.

I know that many of us are idealists at our core, but the world doesn't work on subjective principles. You need to think realistically at times. You want to save money and create abundance in your life? A realistic mindset can help you cut back on unnecessary purchases and useless cravings.

Things do not make us happy. Not deeply, not relevantly. When you catch yourself looking at a cool new gadget and thinking it's going to completely change who you are and how you think, pull yourself back to Earth. Will a new laptop totally make you a better worker or a better person?

If you are honest with yourself, you'll realize that the craving for the object comes from a more profound craving—to feel accepted or good enough. This is the real issue you should treat and maybe invest some money into, not the gadget. If you are okay with yourself, you don't need a tool to complete or upgrade you as a person.

When you find something you think you can't live without, ask yourself why you want it. Then ask yourself why you want it once more. And again. Can this purchase wait? Why must it be purchased right this minute? Oftentimes, you will realize it's an impulse purchase and not needed.

There are some general misconceptions about buying habits—and the tools that make purchases happen. Credit cards don't give you freedom.

Just because you have available credit does not mean you can afford something. When you want something new, it's easy to take out your credit card and swipe it. You don't think about how that purchase will need to be paid off because you are not seeing the money immediately leave your account.

It's a trap. Why save up for something when you can purchase it right now with your credit? But the credit is not yours; it's the credit card company's. The average interest rate on a credit card is over ten percent. That $200 outfit you just bought becomes a lot more if you don't pay it off immediately. This interest will occur daily when you can't pay it by the end of the billing cycle. Depending on your financial situation, it could take you months to pay it off.

If you saved up your money, you could have purchased the outfit with cash and saved yourself the interest. You would have saved money, refrained from getting into debt, and wouldn't have to worry about paying it off later. The best way of saving that money is to not buy a $200 dress when you are short on money in the first place.

Credit cards are not the answer. They restrict you by putting you into debt.

If you struggle with saving money, you aren't the only one. Having savings allows you to live a better financial and personal life. When your finances aren't dragging you down, you are free to accomplish more without the added stress of being in debt.

When you find yourself going into a spending mindset,

remember why you want to save in the first place. Maybe it's to be financially free, or maybe it is to save up and purchase a better car or a newer home. Whatever reasons you have, don't let yourself forget them. Write down the reasons or items you are saving for. This can be done on a piece of paper, or you can make a fun vision board of all you hope to achieve in life by saving.

While there are things you will need to spend money on, anything beyond what is necessary is really a want. You may exclaim, "I need this phone!" But in reality, you want the phone. Learn to separate what you really need and what you want. Your wants can hurt your savings. Take a few days before purchasing items. If it is a want, you will usually forget about it.

Our upbringing can also affect our savings mindset. We may not have the best relationship with money, and may find ourselves spending it after saving for a while. There are a lot of different reasons why this could happen. If you don't address these problems, your financial success will be hard to come by. There are a lot of people who struggle with money problems and have created support groups to help each other.

Progress in accumulating savings can help keep you motivated and excited to continue. You can even reward yourself in relation to how well you are saving. Once you save a certain amount, mark it off and give yourself a small reward like a fun night out. Just don't go too crazy. Give yourself a strict budget you can spend while rewarding yourself. An even better way to celebrate is to enjoy the simple things. Watch some more TV or your favorite movie, bake some cookies, or do other activities that may not require spending money at all. Celebrating your successes is important; just don't forget to keep track of how far you have come.

If you haven't learned more about why you spend money on the things you do, you should look over your purchases and take financial inventory. There's usually a reason we spend money on certain things. Whether this is buying new clothes to make us feel good or purchasing certain items to impress our friends, these are the habits that get us in debt. It's best to know why you spend the money you are spending so you can fix it before spending creates a bigger problem.

To really keep yourself on the saving track, keep educating yourself on your finances. The best thing you can do to help your finances is to research the areas you need help in. Learning and knowing more about money management will help you make the right decisions when the time comes.

New financial information comes out every day, along with ever-changing resources to maximize your savings. Stay updated, ask help from your bank representative often, and stay in the financial zone.

BUDGET

Budgeting sounds "unsexy." You'd think millionaires never do it. It is not true. Millionaires are those people among us who you wouldn't even think about. We get the concept that a true millionaire drives expensive cars, flashes money like in some music videos, and acts in a certain obnoxious manner that drives us crazy, making us think they are some rich douchebag with no feelings.

Some millionaires are like that. But they are a minority, and weirdly, seem to come from the poorer half of "their kind." People with money usually don't show off. They blend in so much, in fact, that you wonder where they are. Fairly often, they are among us.

They don't spend money recklessly, but they have money. And they have money because they are mindful about their spending. They are the people who choose the cheaper parking spot. They are those whose everyday clothes are quality material, but not necessarily high-class branded. They are the Volvo drivers who respect the speed limit.

Some of them were born to be millionaires, but many of them made their own fortune. This latter group had a strict, well-respected budgeting system until, and even after, they reached the mythic seven figures. If you're a millionaire, you already know this. I assume that most readers are just on their way to becoming one, therefore I'll introduce the easiest way to budget.

THE MINT METHOD

Mint is a very compact personal finance site and app. You can sign up for free and set your account up to track your everyday spending. You can set alerts, track and pay bills, and of course, create an online budget.

Mint's budgeting concept lays on the 50/30/20 budgeting rule. The numbers stand for the proportions in monthly spending—essentials, personal spending, and savings. This guideline was created and developed by financial advisors and money masterminds to help you keep your expenses on track. Regardless of which stage of your life are you in, you can greatly benefit by adopting this budgeting system.

If you're in your mid-twenties, just opening your wings as a self-supporting adult, you're very lucky. You're still young. The earlier you start to budget, the better. You have a chance that not many people had when they started their adult life. You can set your financial goals at the very beginning and customize them based on your experience about it.

If you are in your thirties, forties, fifties, or older, don't think you're too late. You can still turn that sinking financial ship around and generate savings and a better life for yourself. Each day spent with reckless spending is a day lost to improve. Improvement starts on the first day. This is why budgeting is so amazing—you don't need long months or years to start benefiting. Better financial conditions begin on the first day. Of course, you'll need even years to accumulate bigger savings depending on your income.

Whether you're young or experienced, try your best to include the good habit of budgeting in your everyday life. The more consistently you do it, the easier and simpler it will become. Feel free to question everything you read in the following budgeting method. Change them here and there, personalize the core concepts to your own needs. Any type of budgeting system is better than none.

In Mint's 50/30/20 rule, fifty percent stays for essentials, thirty percent for personal expenses, and twenty percent for savings. Shortly, these are the percentages of how you should divide a hundred percent of your income. Spending fifty percent for essentials might seem like a high number at first, but considering that it includes everything from your housing bills to your morning coffee, it's actually an accurate percentage.

These are the costs you can't run away from. Everybody pays them in more or less the same percentage. You can try to reduce essential costs, but they might pop out in a different area. Let's say you live in the city center and you pay expensive rent. However, since everything is close to you, the location might save you on travel costs. It also saves you some time. If you live in the suburbs, your monthly rent might be lower, but the savings dwindle on transportation and time.

The most common expenses in the "essentials" category are food, housing-related costs, utility bills, and transportation. I consider phone and internet bills as essential than as personal expenses in the age we're living in. Feel free to exclude them from your essentials list if you disagree. Some people do.

The personal category is the deal-breaker category in your budget. If you choose to live on a short string, you might be able to add all thirty percent to your savings category. In any case, here you can cut the most "useless" spending. Don't feel stressed about feeling the need to spend all thirty percent on your personal needs—that's why this category was created in the first place. Some people have low demands when it comes to "self-defining" costs, and others have higher. If you stay within the percentage given, your budget will still survive. If you want more luxury items in your life rather than save more, it's fine. But don't expect an exponential growth in your savings account.

Experts gave thirty percent for personal needs and twenty percent for savings because there are so many nonessentials that people want. If you think that, for you, savings and planning for the future are more important, feel free to switch the percentage of the two categories.

The most common expenses in the "personal" category are cable TV bills, coffee breaks in a café, makeup, clothing, gym memberships, dining out, other memberships ... I consider extra luxury choices in your essentials to also be a personal expense. For example, renting an apartment in the city center by itself is not a luxury. If you rent the rooftop apartment for a better view, with an extra ten percent rental fee, that's a luxury.

These are only the standard expenses in the personal category. You are the one who can decide what is really an essential or a personal expense for you. If you're a bodybuilder, a gym membership is essential. The key feature you should keep in mind regarding the personal category is that the fewer expenses you have here, the quicker you'll be able to build up savings for a house, car, or to pay down your debts.

The third category in the Mint method is the twenty percent savings. They call it a "get ahead" category. I just nicknamed it your best friend to give you peace of mind. Having savings can grant a feeling of safety. You can be sure that if a car hits you, if you fall ill, or just need to go to a distant relative at the last minute, money won't be a problem.

Some financial gurus suggest putting only ten percent of your income in savings. Indeed, it is better than no savings at all. Compared to that, twenty percent savings might seem like a daring statement to make. Don't forget, you save for yourself, not for another's sake. The more you save today, the more you'll have tomorrow. Taken like that, if you save twenty percent of your monthly income, in five months you'll have one month's salary worth in your savings account. In a year, two months, and so on.

Planning savings into your budget might vary on individual needs. There are two extreme cases: the super rich and the super poor. If you're lucky and inherited two million dollars and put it all in savings, good for you. With two million dollars in your account you could spend all your income on macaroons and still have a decent amount of monthly savings increase on interests. If you have such a low income that you can hardly pay for only your essentials, and you'd risk losing your home if you cut twenty percent for your savings, of course, this is not the right time to think about savings. Think about how to make more money first if you're in that phase of life.

If you're in neither of the two categories above, plan your savings. The best way to estimate how much you can save in reality is after paying off your essentials but not your personal expenses. For example, let's say you want to stick to the twenty percent savings model. After you pay all your essential costs you'll realize that sixty percent of your income is gone. In this case, if you put aside twenty percent for savings, it means you'll have only twenty percent for personal expenses. But if you spend on your personal expenses first, you would have just ten percent for savings. If your goal is to save twenty percent by any means, you'll face a problem, and you wouldn't be able to comply with your budget. This is why the hierarchy of expenses is:

> essentials
> savings
> personal

The most common expenses in the "savings" category are savings plans, emergency funds, debt payments, and retirement savings.

If you are in your twenties, the word "retirement" may sound so foreign and hilarious to even think about it. It still seems an eternity away. Not urgent at all. However, if you take the calculation I made above, in a year you can save two months' worth of salary with twenty percent monthly savings. This means you'll be covered for a year after six years of savings. For five years after thirty years of saving. And this is considering that you never touch your savings during those years. There is compounding interest on your fund the older it gets, but still, nobody became a millionaire on retirement fund interest. If you're a young titan, you might not feel the burning urgency of retirement savings, but you'll be grateful at the age of sixty-five.

Developing good budgeting habits sets you on a good track for a lifetime. The 50/30/20 method is very easily adoptable since it divides based on proportions, not strict numbers. Everybody who has an income can follow it. As your income grows, the proportions still stay the same, they just mean a bigger number.

The proportions are a framework rather than a rule, though. As I emphasized before, you know how you can adjust it to serve your financial interests most effectively. You can always review your self-imposed proportions if you need to, or if anything in your finances or goals change.

Final Words...

Are you ready to kick over the first domino in your habit chain by adopting one of the keystone habits mentioned above? I certainly hope so. Allow your life to take a positive turn with more ease.

Best of luck.
Steven

References

American Psychological Association. Delaying Gratification. American Psychological Association. https://www.apa.org/helpcenter/willpower-gratification.pdf

Carnegie, Dale. How to Win Friends and Influence People. Ebury Digital; New Ed edition. 2010.

Cloud, John. Study: Doodling Helps You Pay Attention. Time. 2009. http://content.time.com/time/health/article/0,8599,1882127,00.html

Duhigg, Charles. The Power of Habit. Cornerstone Digital. 2012.

Fuchs, Eberhard; Flügge, Gabriele. Adult Neuroplasticity: More Than 40 Years of Research. Neural Plasticity. 2014. 1–10. doi:10.1155/2014/541870

Hampton, Debbie. Neuroplasticity: The 10 Fundamentals of Rewiring Your Brain. Reset. 2015. http://reset.me/story/neuroplasticity-the-10-fundamentals-of-rewiring-your-brain/

Kanazawa, Satoshi. Is There Really a Beauty Premium or an Ugliness Penalty on Earnings? Readcube. 2017. http://www.readcube.com/articles/10.1007/s10869-017-9489-6?shared_access_token=1t3KgjzTh7pNlTbKiFeGeve4RwlQNchNByi7wbcMAY5AyXY818SLPa3uGSQOp-H39rZHtxCnFbwns2PYqDYgf6BwMwP8Tf8UPqmSBowGTc-FbG5g4Xo-R9oL4XzkMjWYoeH8lxBnPvl-

NXH01uHEfMZlhTZwqWAJ_ci_so7kM9Zc%3D

Katherine A. MacLean, Emilio Ferrer, Stephen R. Aichele, David A. Bridwell, Anthony P. Zanesco, Tonya L. Jacobs, Brandon G. King, Erika L. Rosenberg, Baljinder K. Sahdra, Phillip R. Shaver, B. Alan Wallace, George R. Mangun, Clifford D. Saron. Intensive Meditation Training Improves Perceptual Discrimination and Sustained Attention. Sage Journals. 2010. http://journals.sagepub.com/doi/abs/10.1177/0956797610371339

Lifelong Learning Council Queensland INC. What Is Lifelong Learning? Lifelong Learning Council Queensland INC. 2016. http://www.llcq.org.au/01_cms/details.asp?ID=12

Rosen, Larry D. PhD. Attention Alert: A Study on Distraction Reveals Some Surprises. Psychology Today. 2012. https://www.psychologytoday.com/blog/rewired-the-psychology-technology/201204/attention-alert-study-distraction-reveals-some

Shellenbarger, Sue. The Power of the Doodle: Improve Your Focus and Memory. The Wall Street Journal. 2014. https://www.wsj.com/articles/the-power-of-the-doodle-improve-your-focus-and-memory-1406675744

Swami, Viren. Furnham, Adrian. Personality and Aesthetic Experience. Research Gate. 2016. https://www.researchgate.net/publication/290653742_Personality_and_aesthetic_experiences

Weir, Kirsten. Power of Self-Control. American Psychological Association. 2012. http://www.apa.org/monitor/2012/01/self-control.aspx

Yates, Diana. Brief Diversions Vastly Improve Focus, Researchers Find. Illinois News Bureau. 2011. https://news.illinois.edu/blog/view/6367/205427

Endnotes

1 Duhigg, Charles. The Power of Habit. Cornerstone Digital. 2012.
2 Duhigg, Charles. The Power of Habit. Cornerstone Digital. 2012.
3 American Psychological Association. Delaying Gratification. American Psychological Association. https://www.apa.org/helpcenter/willpower-gratification.pdf
4 Weir, Kirsten. The Power of Self-Control. American Psychological Association. 2012. http://www.apa.org/monitor/2012/01/self-control.aspx
5 Yates, Diana. Brief Diversions Vastly Improve Focus, Researchers Find. Illinois News Bureau. 2011. https://news.illinois.edu/blog/view/6367/205427
6 Rosen, Larry D. PhD. Attention Alert: A Study on Distraction Reveals Some Surprises. Psychology Today. 2012. https://www.psychologytoday.com/blog/rewired-the-psychology-technology/201204/attention-alert-study-distraction-reveals-some
7 Cloud, John. Study: Doodling Helps You Pay Attention. Time. 2009. http://content.time.com/time/health/article/0,8599,1882127,00.html
8 Shellenbarger, Sue. The Power of the Doodle: Improve Your Focus and Memory. The Wall Street Journal. 2014. https://www.wsj.

com/articles/the-power-of-the-doodle-improve-your-focus-and-memory-1406675744

9   Fuchs, Eberhard; Flügge, Gabriele. Adult Neuroplasticity: More Than 40 Years of Research. Neural Plasticity. 2014. 1–10. doi:10.1155/2014/541870

10 Lifelong Learning Council Queensland INC. What Is Lifelong Learning? Lifelong Learning Council Queensland INC. 2016. http://www.llcq.org.au/01_cms/details.asp?ID=12

11 Hampton, Debbie. Neuroplasticity: The 10 Fundamentals of Rewiring Your Brain. Reset. 2015. http://reset.me/story/neuroplasticity-the-10-fundamentals-of-rewiring-your-brain/

12 Kanazawa, Satoshi. Is There Really a Beauty Premium or an Ugliness Penalty on Earnings? Readcube. 2017. http://www.readcube.com/articles/10.1007/s10869-017-9489-6?shared_access_token=1t3KgjzTh7pNlTbKiFeGeve4RwlQNchNByi7wbcMAY5AyXY818SLPa3uGSQOp-H39rZHtxCnFbwns2PYqDYgf6BwMwP8Tf8UPqmSBowGTc-FbG5g4Xo-R9oL4XzkMjWYoeH8lxBnPvl-NXH01uHEfMZlhTZwqWAJ_ci_so7kM9Zc%3D

13 Swami, Viren. Furnham, Adrian. Personality and aesthetic experience. Research Gate. 2016. https://www.researchgate.net/publication/290653742_Personality_and_aesthetic_experiences

14 Carnegie, Dale. How to win friends and influence people? Ebury Digital; New Ed edition. 2010.

15 Katherine A. MacLean, Emilio Ferrer, Stephen R. Aichele, David A. Bridwell, Anthony P. Zanesco, Tonya L. Jacobs, Brandon G. King, Erika L. Rosenberg, Baljinder K. Sahdra, Phillip R. Shaver, B. Alan Wallace, George R. Mangun, Clifford D. Saron. Intensive Meditation Training Improves Perceptual Discrimination and Sustained Attention. Sage Journals. 2010. http://journals.sagepub.com/doi/abs/10.1177/0956797610371339